Can You See Sasha?

by Katie Dale

illustrated by Ian Smitn

OXFORD
UNIVERSITY PRESS

Seth can not see Sasha the cat.

Can you see Sasha?

That is not Sasha.
It is a quick chick!

Seth dashes to the bank.
He sees a big toad.

It is not Sasha.
It is a duck!

A robin sings high in the oak.

Then Seth sees a tail.

That might be Sasha!

It is not Sasha.
It is Buzz the dog!

Seth checks the sink and bath.

Then he checks his bed.

"I can not see my cat," sighs Seth.

12

Seth peeps at the cat.

Is it Sasha?

15

toad

duck

chick

robin

Encourage the child to read the animal names
and match them to the pictures.